25 ESSENTIALS

TECHNIQUES FOR Smoking

Every Technique Paired with a Recipe

Ardie A. Davis

HARVARD
COMMON
PRESS

Brimming with creative inspiration, how-to projects, and useful information to enrich your everyday life, Quarto Knows is a favorite destination for those pursuing their interests and passions. Visit our site and dig deeper with our books into your area of interest: Quarto Creates, Quarto Cooks, Quarto Homes, Quarto Lives, Quarto Drives, Quarto Explores, Quarto Gifts, or Quarto Kids.

© 2017 Quarto Publishing Group USA Inc.
Text © 2009 by Ardie A. Davis

First Published in 2017
by The Harvard Common Press, an imprint of The Quarto Group,
100 Cummings Center, Suite 265-D, Beverly, MA 01915, USA.
T (978) 282-9590 F (978) 283-2742 QuartoKnows.com

The Harvard Common Press titles are also available at discount for retail, wholesale, promotional, and bulk purchase. For details, contact the Special Sales Manager by email at specialsales@quarto.com or by mail at The Quarto Group, Attn: Special Sales Manager, 401 Second Avenue North, Suite 310, Minneapolis, MN 55401, USA.

21 20 19 18 17   1 2 3 4 5

ISBN: 978-1-55832-878-5

Digital edition published in 2017

Originally found under the following Library of Congress Cataloging-in-Publication Data

Davis, Ardie A.
25 essentials : techniques for smoking
/ Ardie A. Davis.
p. cm.
ISBN 978-1-55832-393-3
(case bound, spiral : alk. paper)
1. Smoked foods. 2. Cookery (Smoked foods) I. Title. II. Title: Twenty-five essentials.
TX609.D38 2009
641.6'16--dc22
2008036449

Design: www.traffic-design.co.uk
Photography: Michael Piazza
Food and Prop Styling: Sally Staub

Printed in China

Contents

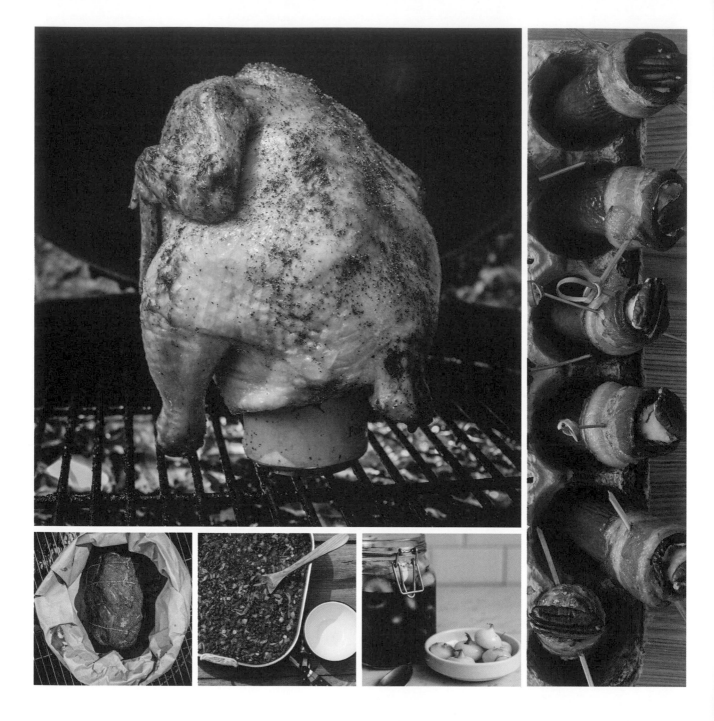

Acknowledgments

All who engage in the art, science, business, or sport of barbecue at its best are standing on the shoulders of past and present pitmasters.

Many past pitmasters have slipped into anonymity, but we still feel their influence. Of those who are not anonymous, my thanks go out to the following who have been of great help and inspiration to me on my barbecue journey:

Paul Kirk, Carolyn Wells, Judith Fertig, Karen Adler, John Willingham, Smoky Hale, John Raven, Bob Lyon, Dennis Hayes, Phil Litman, Rick Browne, Nick Spinelli, Steven Raichlen, Chris Schlesinger, Tana Shupe, Charlie Vergos, to name a few among many.

Thanks also to:

Art Davis, Al Lawson, Jim Quessenberry, Gary Wells, Jack Kay and John Beadle, may they rest in peace.

Special thanks to my wife, Gretchen, for her love and encouragement, and for making possible the time and space in which to do this book.

Finally, a hearty thanks to Judith Fertig (again), Valerie Cimino, and Michele Caterina for a superb job of editing. It was delightful to work with you!

Introduction

Drop the word "barbecue" into any gathering and you'll stir up a hubbub of chatter about who makes it best. Most people think theirs is the best, or that the best is sold at a little rib joint they have frequented in their hometown since childhood.

There's a lot of hype in the world of barbecue. Boasts of "world famous," "legendary," "award winning," and "world champion" abound. Newcomers to barbecue could easily get the impression that the field is too crowded with famous, awardwinning, world-champion legends to make room for more. Don't be discouraged by the hoopla. There is room around the pit for you. You'll find that barbecuers are among the friendliest people on earth. They love to share what they know with anyone who wants to learn.

Mastering the barbecue method of cooking takes a long time. Becoming famous for your barbecue takes even longer. I don't know a single world-famous pitmaster who won fame overnight.

This book is built on the philosophy that every pitmaster should first learn the essentials: fire, smoke, and minimal seasonings. Barbecue as practiced in these pages is a method of cooking meats for several hours, usually at a temperature of 225° to 250°F, in a charcoal or gas grill, cooker, smoker, or pit with wood smoke and hardwood charcoal or charcoal briquets. In barbecue circles we call it the "lowand-slow" method, compared to grilling "hot and fast." For some recipes that don't require a long smoking time, you can use a gas grill, but for real, true barbecue, charcoal is best. Experiencing the flavor of meat cooked with fire and smoke will serve as your touchstone for evaluating barbecue that has been seasoned with herbs, spices, sweeteners, and other seasonings. The barbecue recipes in this book, therefore, 12 are light on seasonings. Pepper, salt, garlic, olive oil, and butter are the mainstays. Although there are many excellent sauces and rubs on the market that go well with barbecue (and you may have your favorite homemade versions as well), I advise using them judiciously, and only after you've tasted unseasoned barbecue. Avoid overpowering the wonderful flavor of real barbecued meat. If a sauce or rub doesn't genuinely complement the flavor of your barbecued meat, don't use it.

Learning the basics of barbecue is simple. Simple, however, doesn't mean easy. After becoming skilled at the fundamentals and putting your knowledge to work at the pit, the more you barbecue, the more you improve and learn. You can do it. So if you dream of becoming a barbecue legend, you'll get there faster by masteringthese basics. Let's get started!

The Essentials of Barbecue

The barbecue method of cooking is simple. It takes some kind of a pit, along with heat from hardwood or hardwood coals or gas. Time and patience also help.

Barbecue is cooked at low temperatures (225° to 250°F) for long periods of time—usually from 4 to 12 or more hours, depending upon the size and composition of the meat. Vegetables, fish, and shellfish can slow smoke in less time. Sometimes, however, you will want to smoke at 350°F—to smoke shellfish, to get a "bark" (also known as a crust or coating) started on pork butt, or to cook a beer-can chicken.

THE MAGIC OF LOW, SLOW HEAT AND SMOKE

You can do wonders with charcoal briquets and wood chips. Hardwood lump charcoal works, but it burns faster and is more expensive than briquets. Slower-burning briquets hold a steady temperature longer, thus requiring fewer times to lift the lid and lose heat.

The most popular woods for adding smoke flavor are:

- **Hickory, oak, pecan, maple, sassafras, cherry, grapevines, whiskey or wine barrel wood:** For medium smoke flavor.

- **Mesquite:** For heavier smoke flavor.

- **Alder, apple, peach:** For somewhat sweet or milder smoke flavor.

For each recipe, I suggest woods that are appropriate to the food. Mesquite on chicken, for example, would be too bitter, while alder on beef would be too mild.

For a kettle grill, you will want to use wood chips. Twice-soaked in water and drained, chips are the easiest to use and are my preference. The first soaking can be as short as 20 minutes or as long as overnight. Drain the water from the first soak, cover the chips with fresh water for another 20 minutes, and drain again before scattering on the hot coals. If you're using a gas grill, you'll want to pack dry wood chips into a metal container that will go as close to a burner as you can get it. You don't want to scatter dry chips on gas grill burners, as the chips can clog the burners.

The amount of wood chips I specify in each recipe will yield enough smoke to flavor your food during the first 45 minutes to 1 hour of cooking. There is no need to add more smoke after that. Barbecue cooked with too much smoke will taste bitter.

SMOKERS

Barbecuers call their specially designed slow-smoking units by a lot of different names—pits, cookers, smokers, rigs—and I'll use them all in this book. With an indirect fire, wood chips, and a lid, you can turn just about any grill into a smoker, but I prefer that icon of the backyard, the 22½-inch charcoal kettle grill. It's basic, but it's really all you need.

You can go for a bullet-shaped smoker (charcoal, gas, or electric), a bigger rig with an offset firebox, inexpensive home-built pits, elaborate rigs costing thousands of dollars, or a ceramic smoker like the Big Green Egg. You can also use your gas grill as a smoker for some things that only take about an hour to smoke. But imagine doing a brisket on a gas grill for 12 hours—and how many times you'd have to change the cylinder! The best way to learn the basics is on the less expensive, less complex charcoal kettle grill.

ROTISSERIE AND SPIT COOKING

Cooking skewered meat near hot hardwood coals is a wonderful way to get moist, flavorful results. Some cookers come equipped with rotisserie adapters. Others can be rigged up from creative combinations of gears, bicycle chains, and an electric motor, like the one my dad made for his homemade brick barbecue pit. The rotisserie method can be used for meat cuts ranging from roasts to whole animals. It's a good idea for beginners to master the technique with smaller cuts of meat or whole chickens before tackling anything bigger.

Two important tips on success with your rotisserie: Make sure the meat is balanced and firmly secured to the rod and that its weight does not exceed the maximum number of pounds recommended for your rig.

BASIC TOOL KIT FOR PITMASTERS

Once you have your smoker of choice, then it's time to make sure you have all the essential tools. Carloads of gear and gadgets clamor for the attention of barbecue cooks. Some are endorsed by celebrity chefs. Now and then you'll see a gadget you can't resist. If you already have the essential tools, go ahead and give in to temptation. If it doesn't work to your satisfaction, toss it. Here are the basic things you will need:

- **Sharp knives:** The most important prep tool is a set of good-quality, sharpened knives, including the four indispensable ones: butcher, carving, chef's, and boning knives. If you like to serve chopped pork shoulder or beef brisket, a sharp cleaver is also essential.

- **Long-handled fork:** You can insert this in a pork butt or brisket and twist to check for tenderness toward the end of smoking.

- **Long-handled tongs:** Stainless-steel spring-loaded tongs work best. They are useful for spreading or moving hot coals in the grill, in addition to handling food on the grill.

- **Cutting boards:** My preference is for boards made of hardwood or bamboo. I recommend having two cutting boards—one for meat and one for fruits and vegetables. Thoroughly clean the cutting board between uses.

- **Rimmed pan:** A rimmed pan—about 12 x 16 inches in size—is important for carrying raw meat to your cooker and cooked meat from your cooker. Thoroughly clean the pan, of course, before putting the cooked meat in it, or have two: one for raw meat and one for cooked. If you plan to use your pan for marinating or brining meat, get a stainless-steel or glass pan that won't interact with acids and salts.

- **Thermometers:** You'll need a grill thermometer for monitoring the temperature inside the cooker and a meat thermometer for checking the internal temperature of the meat as it cooks.

- **Welder's gloves:** I use leather welder's gloves, available in hardware stores or online, to protect my hands from the heat of the cooker. Wear them when dumping hot coals from the charcoal chimney to the bottom grate (also known as the fire grate), when brushing a grill over hot coals, and at all other times when your hands are near fire.

- **Charcoal chimney (for charcoal grills):** This is the fire-starting method of choice for most experienced cooks. See "Building the Fire" (opposite) for how to use one of these inexpensive and durable aluminized-steel starters.

- **Electric charcoal starters:** These are also popular, especially in places where smoke from burning newspaper is objectionable.

BUILDING THE FIRE

For each recipe in this book, you'll need to start an indirect fire in your grill for smoking. The food will be placed opposite from the heat and will cook as a result of the high temperature inside the grill and not from being on top of flames.

If using a charcoal grill, start your fire using a charcoal chimney. Place your charcoal chimney on a nonflammable surface and fill the top of the chimney to the desired level with briquets. Slightly tip the chimney over and stuff one to two sheets of crumpled newspaper into the convex-shaped bottom. Place the chimney on your lower grill grate and light the paper with a match. In 15 to 20 minutes, your briquets should be glowing, ashed over, and ready to spread over the bottom of the grill. Wearing welder's gloves, remove the grill grate and dump the hot coals into the bottom of your grill. Using a grill spatula or long-handled fork, bank the coals onto one half of the grill and spread them out evenly in that half.

Use lighter fluid or pretreated briquets as a last resort, and make sure coals are free of lighter residue before grilling.

For a gas grill, simply turn on one or two of the burners, depending on how your gas grill is configured.

MANAGING THE FIRE

Learning to manage your fire and maintain a fairly constant 225° to 250°F cooking temperature is the secret of good barbecue. To adjust the temperature on a closed charcoal grill, open the vents wider to increase the temperature and narrow the vents to decrease it. To adjust the temperature on a gas grill, simply turn the knob.

CLEANING THE COOKER

A clean cooker is important as a matter of food safety and food flavor. Don't let residue from previously cooked meats taint your freshly cooked meat with bitter or "off" flavors. A wire welder's brush or grill brush will remove cooking residue from the grate. I use a stainless-steel spatula to scrape away excess creosote and fat buildup in the cooker.

When my cooker needs a major cleaning, I apply oven cleaner or a grease-cutting liquid, followed by a jet spray with a garden hose to remove all chemical residue.

SERVES 4

Tuscan Smoke-Marinated Cipollini Onions

Cipolle alla brace—smoked, pickled spring onions—crank up an antipasto platter from "good" to "remarkable!" Instead of onions, you can also lightly smoke and then marinate stemmed mushrooms, bell pepper strips, or even baby artichokes for an Italian take on barbecued appetizers. Fresh cipollini onions are also good grilled kebab-style with chicken, duck, pork, or lamb. This recipe recalls some favorite culinary moments at Montestigliano, an agritourism complex close to Siena, in Tuscany. For a true Tuscan flavor, choose oak or apple wood, since these are the preferred smoking woods in Tuscany and they will make your onions taste most authentic.

Suggested wood:
Oak or apple

INGREDIENTS

8 ounces yellow cipollini onions, ends trimmed and outer layers removed

½ cup wood chips, soaked in water and drained, or 1 cup dry wood chips for a gas grill

2 cups balsamic vinegar

¼ cup extra-virgin olive oil

METHOD

1. Fill your charcoal chimney three-quarters full with briquets, set the chimney on the bottom grill grate, and light, or prepare a fire in your smoker. For a gas grill, turn half the burners to medium. Spray a large piece of heavy-duty aluminum foil or a disposable aluminum pan with the olive oil and arrange the onions on it.

2. When the coals are ready, dump them into the bottom of your grill, and spread them evenly across half. Scatter the drained wood chips on the hot coals, or put the dry wood chips in a metal container and place as close as possible to a burner on a gas grill. Place the onions on the indirect-heat side of the grill. When the smoke starts to rise, close the lid.

3. Smoke the onions at 225° to 250°F for 15 minutes or until they have a mild, smoky aroma and are soft when you pierce them gently with a sharp knife. Place the onions in a 1-quart Mason jar. Cover the onions with the balsamic vinegar and olive oil; screw the lid on the jar and shake it to mix the contents. The onions will keep in the refrigerator for up to 1 month.

2 | SMOKING WHOLE VEGETABLES
SERVES 4

Whole Smoked Garlic

Your guests will enjoy the fun and flavors they get from squeezing sweet, soft, smoked garlic from a clove, spreading it on a baguette slice, and topping it with a slice of goat cheese and tomato. The mere thought of it makes me hungry! Because garlic starts out pungent but then gets sweet as it slowly smokes, choose a medium-flavor wood. When preparing the garlic heads for smoking, take care to slice off only enough to make it easy to squeeze the smoked garlic from each clove. You can also use this technique with whole, cored tomatoes, small new potatoes, or stemmed mushrooms—just smoke until the vegetables are softened and have a good, smoky aroma.

Suggested wood:
Apple, pecan, or hickory

INGREDIENTS

4 whole heads garlic, ½ inch sliced off the pointed top of each

⅓ cup wood chips, soaked in water and drained, or 1 cup dry wood chips for a gas grill

1 whole-grain baguette, sliced

One 7½-ounce goat cheese log (I like Vermont chèvre)

1 medium-size ripe tomato, sliced, or 8 cherry tomatoes

Fine sea salt and freshly ground black pepper

METHOD

1. Fill your charcoal chimney three-quarters full with briquets, set the chimney on the bottom grill grate, and light, or prepare a fire in your smoker. For a gas grill, turn half the burners to medium. Spray a 6 x 6-inch piece of heavy-duty aluminum foil or a disposable aluminum pan with olive or canola oil and arrange the garlic on it.

2. When the coals are ready, dump them into the bottom of your grill, and spread them evenly across half. Scatter the drained wood chips on the hot coals, or put the dry wood chips in a metal container and place as close as possible to a burner on a gas grill. Place the garlic on the indirect-heat side of the grill. When the smoke starts to rise, close the lid.

3. Smoke the garlic at 225° to 250°F for 45 minutes or until it has a mild, smoky aroma. To serve, set out the smoked garlic, baguette slices, goat cheese, and tomatoes. Guests can squeeze out the smoked garlic cloves and spread them onto the bread, along with the cheese, then top with a slice of tomato and salt and pepper to taste.

SERVES 6

Smoke-Baked Barbecue Chile Pie

Smoke baking is a great technique to use for garlic bread, pizzas, quiche, or a savory breakfast casserole—whenever you want to bake and get a hit of smoky flavor at the same time. You can smoke bake using a charcoal grill, gas grill, or a traditional smoker with a smoking temperature you can control (water smokers have a set temperature of 225° to 250°F and will not work for this recipe).

When chiles from Hatch, New Mexico, come to market in August, I stock up on enough to roast and freeze for chile pies, pots of Southwestern chili, and batches of salsa through the winter months. You can substitute other varieties of chiles (or bell peppers for a less spicy result) in this recipe and experiment with additional ingredients, such as a garnish of chopped scallions, cilantro, or parsley. A teaspoon of your favorite chili seasoning blend or barbecue dry rub could add a special accent. If you can't get Hatch chile peppers, no problem. Buy fresh green Anaheim peppers and fire roast them at home. For a true Southwestern flavor use the heavier mesquite wood—very sparingly here—or pecan. This is a great dish for a light supper or an outdoor brunch.

Suggested wood:
Pecan or mesquite

INGREDIENTS

1 frozen prepared deep-dish pie crust

8 ounces fire-roasted mild Hatch or other chile peppers, seeded and sliced into strips of varying size (see Note)

8 ounces shredded cheddar–Monterey Jack cheese blend

¼ cup chopped Texas sweet or Vidalia onion

½ teaspoon olive oil

4 large eggs, beaten

¼ cup wood chips, soaked in water and drained, or ½ cup dry wood chips for a gas grill

4 ounces hickory- or maple-smoked bacon, cooked until crisp and chopped

Note: Fire roast the chiles by grilling them over hot coals until the skins blacken, then remove the papery skin, seeds, and membrane. (You should wear food-preparation gloves for this because the oil from hot chiles will stick to your hands. If you rub your eyes or other sensitive areas after working with the chiles, it can be painful. If the chiles are mild, however, gloves aren't necessary.)

METHOD

1. Fill your charcoal chimney with briquets, set the chimney on the bottom grill grate, and light, or prepare a fire in your smoker. For a gas grill, turn half the burners to high.

2. Line the bottom and sides of the pie crust with the chile pepper strips, reserving a few to garnish the top of the pie. Top with the cheese, spreading it out evenly over the bottom of the crust.

3. In a small sauté pan over medium heat, sauté the onions in the olive oil until softened, about 3 minutes. In a medium-size bowl, combine the eggs and onion, then pour the mixture over the cheese. Arrange the reserved chile pepper strips on the top of the pie.

4. When the coals are ready, dump them into the bottom of your grill, and spread them evenly across half. Scatter the drained wood chips on the hot coals, or put the dry wood chips in a metal container and place as close as possible to a burner on a gas grill. Place the pie on the indirect-heat side of the grill. When the smoke starts to rise, close the lid.

5. Smoke bake the pie at 350°F for 40 to 45 minutes or until the crust has browned, the filling has set, and the pie has a mild, smoky aroma. Sprinkle with the bacon before serving.

SERVES 4

Smoked Stuffed Chile Peppers

Chile "poppers"—just pop 'em in your mouth—are on many restaurant menus, and they're easy to prepare in your own backyard. They need to smoke at a higher temperature so the bacon wrapped around the outside of the chile gets cooked through. Although higher-heat smoking is technically not considered low-and-slow traditional barbecue, it does have its place in recipes like this one (and for people who use a ceramic smoker, which automatically smokes at a higher temperature). At a lower temperature, the bacon won't crisp up. You can also use this technique to smoke other bacon-wrapped appetizers like shrimp, water chestnuts, or green bean bundles. If you like, substitute goat cheese, garlic-and-herb cream cheese, or even pimiento cheese spread for the cream cheese and cheddar. You can also use almonds or walnuts instead of the pecans, or omit the nuts.

These poppers are so addictive that you can make a meal out of them! They are slightly fiery, but even friends who describe themselves as heat-intolerant have devoured these and raved about them. Jalapeños of any size will do, but the bigger ones hold more flavor and are easier to fill with cheese. I use a swivel-blade potato peeler or a paring knife to core the peppers. And remember to wear disposable food-handling gloves when touching fresh jalapeños, because the oil from hot chiles will stick to your hands. If you rub your eyes or other sensitive areas after working with the chiles, it can be painful. If the chiles are mild, however, gloves aren't necessary.

You can buy metal chile popper racks, but you can also use a cardboard egg carton. At 350°F, the carton won't burn and you can simply throw it away when you're done. Another big plus to using an egg carton is that the carton absorbs bacon fat. This means no grease flare-ups. You can enhance the hickory or maple wood smoke flavor in the bacon by using that type of wood for your fire, or you can add a little different flavor to your poppers by using apple, oak, or pecan.

Suggested wood:

Hickory or maple

INGREDIENTS

8 ounces cream cheese or Neufchâtel cheese, at room temperature

½ cup shredded sharp cheddar cheese

12 large jalapeño chiles (green, red, or both), cored and seeded

1 empty cardboard egg carton, lid removed, or a metal jalapeño popper rack

12 pecan halves, toasted (see Note)

8 ounces thin-sliced smoked bacon

½ cup wood chips, soaked in water and drained, or 1 cup dry wood chips for a gas grill

METHOD

1. To make the popper filling, combine the cheeses in a medium-size bowl and stir them together with a fork. Put the cheese mixture in a gallon-size zipper-top plastic bag and cut a small hole in one corner of the bag. Squeeze each jalapeño full of the cheese mixture. Place the cheese-filled jalapeños in the egg carton. Push a pecan half into each pepper. Wrap a half strip of bacon around each jalapeño and secure with a toothpick.

2. Fill your charcoal chimney with briquets, set the chimney on the bottom grill grate, and light, or prepare a fire in your smoker. For a gas grill, turn half the burners to high.

3. When the coals are ready, dump them into the bottom of your grill, and spread them evenly across half. Scatter the drained wood chips on the hot coals, or put the dry wood chips in a metal container and place as close as possible to a burner on a gas grill. Place the jalapeños on the indirect-heat side of the grill. When the smoke starts to rise, close the lid.

4. Smoke the peppers at 350°F for 1 hour and 15 minutes or until the bacon is cooked and the jalapeños have a smoky aroma.

Note: I toast my pecans for more flavor before inserting them into the jalapeños. To toast, melt 1 teaspoon unsalted butter in a small cast-iron skillet over medium heat. Add the pecans and cook, stirring, until slightly browned.

SERVES 6

Alder-Smoked Salmon Fillet

Hot-smoked salmon is more moist and tender than the cold-smoked variety. Serve this at a weekend brunch or for a Friday night fish dinner. The leftovers make a wonderful smoked salmon spread. Alder is the traditional wood for smoking in the Pacific Northwest—it's mild, aromatic, and great with salmon. I also like a combination of a fruitwood, such as apple or peach, with medium-flavored hickory or pecan. If you decide to experiment, choose a sweeter wood for smoking salmon, one that will not overpower the natural sweetness of the fish.

This hot-smoking technique works for any type of fish fillet. You can't go wrong matching a fish with a wood from its region; for example, try Southern catfish and hickory, halibut or Arctic char and alder, Florida grouper and oak, New England bluefish and maple.

Suggested wood:
 Alder or a combination of apple and hickory

INGREDIENTS

One 3-pound salmon fillet, preferably skin-on

1 tablespoon extra-virgin olive oil

½ teaspoon fine sea salt

1 teaspoon freshly ground black pepper

½ cup wood chips, soaked in water and drained, or 1 cup dry wood chips for a gas grill

Fresh dill sprigs for garnish

Lemon wedges for garnish

METHOD

1. Fill your charcoal chimney with briquets, set the chimney on the bottom grill grate, and light, or prepare a fire in your smoker. For a gas grill, turn half the burners to medium. Rub the salmon on both sides with the olive oil and sprinkle with the salt and pepper.

2. When the coals are ready, dump them into the bottom of your grill, and spread them evenly across half. Scatter the drained wood chips on the hot coals, or put the dry wood chips in a metal container and place as close as possible to a burner on a gas grill. Place the salmon on the grill grate on the indirect-heat side of the grill. When the smoke starts to rise, close the lid.

3. Smoke the salmon at 225° to 250°F for 45 to 60 minutes or until the fish begins to flake when tested with a fork in the thickest part and has a smoky aroma. Garnish with fresh dill and lemon wedges.

SERVES 4

Vine-Smoked Trout

Trout rule the mountain streams of America. I remember the fantastic flavor of freshly caught trout in Wyoming cooked over a campfire. They were so delicious, we had trout for breakfast, lunch, and dinner. This recipe echoes that experience, sans the stinging nettles and porcupines. If you like, you could also stuff the trout with an herb or horseradish butter, fresh lemon slices, or a cornbread stuffing.

As for the smoking, for trout I prefer the sweeter smoke flavor of alder or even grapevine, which you can gather from the wild or buy as prepackaged wood chips. I use them dry in this recipe, as the trout doesn't take long to smoke. This recipe works for any whole, cleaned fish; the rule of thumb for smoking is 30 minutes per pound at 225° to 250°F.

Suggested wood:
Grapevine or alder

INGREDIENTS

4 whole trout, about 1½ to 2 pounds each, cleaned

Canola oil for brushing

Fine sea salt and freshly ground black pepper to taste

½ cup dry wood chips

Fresh rosemary or sage leaves for garnish

Fresh lemon wedges for garnish

METHOD

1. Fill your charcoal chimney with briquets, set the chimney on the bottom grill grate, and light, or prepare a fire in your smoker. For a gas grill, turn half the burners to medium. Brush the trout all over with canola oil and sprinkle with salt and pepper.

2. When the coals are ready, dump them into the bottom of your grill, and spread them evenly across half. Scatter the wood chips on the hot coals, or place them in a metal container as close as possible to a burner on a gas grill. Place the trout on the grill grate on the indirect-heat side of the grill. When the smoke starts to rise, close the lid.

3. Smoke the trout at 225° to 250°F for 45 to 60 minutes or until the fish begins to flake when tested with a fork in the thickest part and has a smoky aroma. Garnish with rosemary or sage leaves and lemon wedges.

SERVES 4

Barbecued Shrimp Pasta Salad with Citrus Vinaigrette

Smoked shrimp can be served any number of ways—with barbecue sauce in a quesadilla, with cocktail sauce as an appetizer, or in hot or cold pasta dishes. Here is my favorite take on slow-smoked shrimp. I prefer to smoke shrimp in the shell so the shrimp stays moist. I like a hearty smoke flavor like hickory with them, and I use dry chips because the shrimp smokes quickly. You can also use corncobs as your "wood," which turns the shrimp a golden hue.

To smoke shrimp, you can thread the shrimp onto a skewer, arrange them in a disposable aluminum pan, or put them directly on the grill grate. You can also smoke large sea scallops or oysters on the half shell this way—cook them until they're opaque and just firm. Mussels or oysters in the shell need a higher heat to pop open; squid and octopus will get tough and are better when grilled quickly.

Suggested wood:
Hickory or corncobs

INGREDIENTS

¼ cup dry wood chips

16 jumbo shrimp in their shells

½ cup freshly squeezed orange juice

¼ cup freshly squeezed lemon juice

Zest of 1 orange and 1 lemon

1 cup canola oil

2 garlic cloves, minced

2 tablespoons Dijon mustard

2 tablespoons grated Parmesan cheese

2 scallions, chopped

2 tablespoons chopped fresh flat-leaf parsley

1 pound whole-wheat penne, cooked according to package directions

Chopped scallions or fresh flat-leaf parsley for garnish

METHOD

1. Fill your charcoal chimney with briquets, set the chimney on the bottom grill grate, and light, or prepare a fire in your smoker. For a gas grill, turn half the burners to high.

2. When the coals are ready, dump them into the bottom of your grill, and spread them evenly across half. Scatter the wood chips on the hot coals, or place them in a metal container as close as possible to a burner on a gas grill. Place the shrimp on the grill grate on the indirect-heat side of the grill. When the smoke starts to rise, close the lid.

3. Smoke the shrimp at 350°F for 7 to 10 minutes or until opaque. When cool enough to handle, peel and devein the shrimp. Bring the shrimp indoors while you make the pasta salad or refrigerate them until ready to serve.

4. Combine the orange and lemon juices, orange and lemon zests, canola oil, garlic, mustard, Parmesan, scallions, and parsley in a quart-size jar. Place the lid on the jar and shake to mix thoroughly. Pour the mixture on the cooked pasta and toss. To serve, arrange 4 shrimp on each serving of pasta, and garnish with the scallions or parsley.

8 | SMOKING BRISKET

SERVES 8

Braggin' Rights Brisket

Slow smoking a beef brisket until tender and flavorful takes time and patience. If, after hours of cooking, your brisket is still tough, don't be discouraged. Most likely it didn't cook long enough or it was cooked at a temperature that was too high and it got too dry. It took me a long time to master smoking brisket. Now I can save you some time, expense, and frustration with this simple technique.

To start, buy a whole, untrimmed brisket. I go for the cheapest, toughest brisket in the meat case. I've never been disappointed with the cheaper grade. Untrimmed is important, because fat is essential for a tender brisket. Some cooks age the brisket on the bottom shelf of the refrigerator for a week or more. I don't. Second, don't try any fancy marinade, rub, or baste until you've cooked a brisket with this simple salt-and-pepper rub.

After that, jazzier rubs and/or bastes are your choice. Third, be prepared: You'll need at least 10 pounds of charcoal briquets and a lot of vigilance in managing the temperature to see you through to the end. A 10-pound brisket can take up to 12 hours to cook; larger briskets take as long as 15 to 20 hours. The rule of thumb is 1½ to 2 hours of slow-smoking time per pound of meat. The brisket will be done way before it's tender. And don't even think about using a gas grill! Seasoned boiled red potatoes, smashed and mixed with smoke-roasted garlic (page 24), and a grilled vegetable medley make good sides.

Suggested wood:
Mesquite, pecan, apple, hickory, or a blend of woods

INGREDIENTS

One 8- to 10-pound brisket

2 tablespoons fine sea salt

¼ cup freshly ground black pepper

1 cup wood chips, soaked in water and drained

Note: *My kettle grills will go 4 to 6 hours before needing more coals. Each cooker—even the same brand and model—is different. Get to know yours.*

METHOD

1. Fill your charcoal chimney with briquets, set the chimney on the bottom grill grate, and light, or prepare a fire in your smoker. Oil the grill grate. Sprinkle the brisket with the salt and pepper.

2. When the coals are ready, dump them into the bottom of your grill, and spread them evenly across half. Scatter the wood chips on the hot coals. Place the brisket, fat side up, on the indirect-heat side. When the smoke starts to rise, close the lid. Place a candy thermometer in the lid vent of a charcoal grill or smoker. Control the temperature by opening and closing the bottom vents. To raise the temperature, open the vents more; to cool things down, close the vents a bit.

3. Smoke the brisket at 225° to 250°F, adding more briquets (but not wood) at 3- to 4-hour intervals or whenever required to keep the temperature constant (see Note). Plan on smoking the brisket for 10 to 12 hours or until a meat thermometer inserted into the thickest part registers 165°F and a meat fork inserted into the center and given a twist will shred the meat. (Many cooks wrap the brisket in aluminum foil after 6 to 8 hours and leave it in foil for the duration of the cooking time, a technique called the "Texas Crutch," but some say the foil turns the brisket into "pot roast." I have used aluminum foil, but am now weaned from it. Learn how to cook a brisket without foil and you'll never need or want to try it with foil.)

4. Trim the excess fat before slicing the meat. Separate the lower brisket flat from the upper point. Cut the meat against the grain. Texans like thick slices. Kansas Citians like thin slices.

SERVES 4

Barbecued Short Ribs with Olive Oil Baste

Some barbecuers use a baste as a matter of course—melted butter or oil blended with flavorings such as honey, black coffee, or fruit juice. The purpose of a baste is to keep food moist during low-and-slow smoking, whereas a liquid concoction called a mop is brushed onto the meat like a baste, but instead is used to take away some of the fat that comes to the surface as the meat cooks. Kansas Citians have been known to baste their lean ribs with honey and melted butter; Canadian barbecuers might brush their barbecuing salmon with maple syrup–laced butter. North Carolinians mop their slow-smoking pork with simple white or cider vinegar to remove some of the "porky," fatty flavor that can interfere with the flavor of meat, smoke, and spice. Texans do the same with brisket, using strong black coffee as a mop.

For this recipe, choose thick and meaty short ribs, one or two per serving, depending upon the size of the ribs and the appetites of your guests. Seasoned pinto beans and a colorful slaw make excellent side dishes.

Suggested wood:
Pecan, oak, or hickory

INGREDIENTS

4 pounds meaty short ribs

½ cup to 1 cup extra-virgin olive oil, as desired

2 tablespoons freshly ground black pepper

1 teaspoon fine sea salt

½ teaspoon granulated garlic

1 cup wood chips, soaked in water and drained

Tomato-based barbecue sauce for serving

METHOD

1. Fill your charcoal chimney with briquets, set the chimney on the bottom grill grate, and light, or prepare a fire in your smoker. For a gas grill, turn half the burners to high. Oil the grill grate. Using a paring knife or needlenose pliers, strip the membrane from the bone side of the ribs. Brush the ribs with half of the olive oil, and sprinkle lightly with the pepper, salt, and granulated garlic.

2. When the coals are ready, dump them into the bottom of your grill, and spread them evenly across half. Scatter the wood chips on the hot coals or place them in a metal container as close as possible to a burner on a gas grill. Place the ribs, bone side down, on the indirect-heat side. When the smoke starts to rise, close the lid. Place a candy thermometer in the lid vent of a charcoal grill or smoker.

3. Smoke the ribs at 225° to 250°F for 45 to 60 minutes, or until the meat has pulled away from the bone, brushing them with the remaining olive oil after the first half hour. For a crusty bark (also known as a crust or coating), first grill both the meaty and bone sides directly over coals or flames for 5 minutes each, then move the ribs to the indirect-heat side to finish smoking. Remove the ribs from the grill and let rest, covered, for 15 minutes. Serve with a tomato-based barbecue sauce on the side.

SERVES 6 to 8

Smoked Prime Rib

The most difficult part of cooking a standing rib roast is paying for it. Save it for special occasions when you have something big to celebrate but don't have all day to cook. Once you've slow-smoked a standing rib roast, you'll never put one in the oven again, I promise. This recipe features a simple slather, which is a mixture of flavorings (usually without sweeteners) that you can brush on the exterior of the meat to keep it moist and help it get a good bark (also known as a crust or coating). Some examples of simple slathers are American mustard over a pork butt or a combination of Dijon mustard and mayonnaise over a salmon fillet to be smoked. For a robust rib roast, use a heavier wood-smoke flavor like mesquite, or get a medium smoke flavor from pecan, apple, cherry, oak, or hickory wood. This rib roast smokes for 3 hours, so it's better to cook this on a charcoal grill/ smoker or water smoker than a gas grill.

Suggested wood:
Mesquite (use half as much as the other woods), pecan, apple, or cherry

INGREDIENTS

¼ cup extra-virgin olive oil

1 tablespoon freshly ground black pepper

1 tablespoon granulated garlic

½ teaspoon fine sea salt

One 3-pound standing rib roast, ribs cut away from the bones, attached at the wide end, and secured with string

½ cup mesquite or 1 cup other wood chips, soaked in water and drained

METHOD

1. Fill your charcoal chimney with briquets, set the chimney on the bottom grill grate, and light, or prepare a fire in your smoker. Oil the grill grate. In a bowl, combine the olive oil, pepper, granulated garlic, and salt and stir to blend. Use your hands or a basting brush to slather the rib roast with this mixture.

2. When the coals are ready, dump them into the bottom of your grill, and spread them evenly across half. Scatter the wood chips on the hot coals. Place the roast, fat side up, on the indirect-heat side. When the smoke starts to rise, close the lid. Place a candy thermometer in the lid vent of a charcoal grill or smoker.

3. Smoke the ribs at 225° to 250°F. After 2 hours, add more coals if necessary. At this point, using clean welder's gloves or long-handled tongs, turn the roast completely around so that the opposite side is closest to the coals. Close the lid and cook for 1 more hour. After 3 hours, the roast should be tender and juicy, slightly beyond medium-rare, about 140°F. When it has reached your desired level of doneness, remove it from the smoker and let it sit for 15 minutes before slicing. Slice the rib bones off first before slicing meat portions.

SERVES 8

Grilled 'n' Smoked Beef Tenderloin

Marked from the grill but with a savory scent of smoke, this beef tenderloin is king of the special occasion. And, happily for the barbecuer with an indirect fire, you can get both from the same piece of equipment. This technique also works well for pork tenderloin or lamb loin. Grill directly over the hot coals to get some good grill marks on the exterior of the meat, then place it on the indirect-heat side, add the wood chips, and smoke. Keep it simple with seasonings so you can really taste the smoke. Beef tenderloin is milder in flavor than beefier brisket, so a little mesquite smoke will go a long way. Pecan, cherry, apple, hickory, or oak will also work. Serve this with grilled or steamed asparagus and homemade mashed potatoes. The longer smoking time—at least 2 hours—makes smoking this on a gas grill impractical.

Suggested wood:
Mesquite (use half the amount of the other woods), pecan, or cherry

INGREDIENTS

One 4-pound whole beef tenderloin, trimmed

2 tablespoons extra-virgin olive oil

Fine sea salt and freshly ground black pepper

½ cup mesquite or 1 cup other wood chips, soaked in water and drained

METHOD

1. Fill your charcoal chimney with briquets, set the chimney on the bottom grill grate, and light, or prepare a fire in your smoker. Oil the grill grate. Brush the beef with the olive oil; sprinkle lightly with salt and pepper.

2. When the coals are ready, dump them into the bottom of your grill, and spread them evenly across half. Place the tenderloin directly over the coals and grill, turning every 1 to 2 minutes, until you have good grill marks all over. Transfer the meat to the indirect-heat side.

3. Scatter the wood chips on the hot coals. When the smoke starts to rise, close the lid. Place a candy thermometer in the lid vent of a charcoal grill or smoker.

4. Smoke the tenderloin at 225° to 250°F for 2½ to 3 hours, until the meat registers 135°F for rare or to your desired doneness. Remove from the grill and let rest, covered, for 15 minutes before carving.

SERVES 8

Classic Barbecued Spareribs

Tough, meaty spareribs from the side of the hog are the cheapest and thus the best to slow smoke. You can slow smoke more naturally tender baby back ribs (from along the backbone), but there's something really satisfying about turning a tough ol' slab o' spareribs into something to brag about. I look for meaty ribs without any exposed bone—no "shiners." If your ribs are frozen, thaw them in the refrigerator.

This technique involves a 3-step process: trim, skin, and smoke. Some barbecuers like to marinate their ribs before smoking; others like to add a zesty rub. Try ribs this simple way first, then go chase your moonbeam. When you want to cook several slabs of ribs and your grill can't accommodate them horizontally, invest in a rib rack, which is like a toast rack, but for ribs. Ribs smoke just as well vertically as they do horizontally. You can also stack them, one on top of the other; if you stack, change the position of the ribs every 45 minutes. I like a sweeter fruitwood smoke for ribs or that old standby, hickory. Because the ribs need to smoke for a minimum of 3 hours, this recipe is not for a gas grill.

Suggested wood:
Apple, cherry, or hickory

INGREDIENTS

2 full slabs pork spareribs

½ cup freshly ground black pepper

2 tablespoons fine sea salt

1 teaspoon granulated garlic

½ cup canola oil

1 cup wood chips, soaked in water and drained

Barbecue sauce of your choice for serving

METHOD

1. To trim the spareribs, place them bone side up on a cutting board. Using a sharp butcher knife, slice off the flap of meat and save it. Next, if there's a bone on the upper part of the widest side of the rib, cut it off and save that as well (see Note). If you like symmetry, trim the thin end off the slab to make a slanted rectangle.

2. To skin the spareribs, use a table knife, screwdriver, or the handle of a teaspoon to push under the membrane and lift it enough for you to get a grip on it. Pull the membrane off with needlenose pliers or a wad of paper towels and discard. Removing the membrane makes for more tender ribs and allows the smoke to penetrate the meat better. It's okay if some remains.

3. Combine the pepper, salt, and granulated garlic in a small bowl to make a rub.

4. After the ribs are trimmed and skinned, rub both sides with the canola oil and sprinkle with the rub. Set aside while you build your fire.

5. Fill your charcoal chimney with briquets, set the chimney on the bottom grill grate, and light, or prepare a fire in your smoker. Oil the grill grate.

6. When the coals are ready, dump them into the bottom of your grill, and spread evenly across half. Scatter the wood chips on the hot coals. Place the ribs across from the coals on the indirect-heat side of the grill, racked or stacked if necessary. If your rib rack is too high for the lid to fit all the way down when ribs are racked, arrange the coals on both sides of the bottom of the grill and place the rack in the middle of the grill grate. Be sure to position the rib rack so that the rib meat is not directly above the hot coals. When the smoke starts to rise, close the lid. Place a candy thermometer in the lid vent.

7. Smoke the ribs at 225° to 250°F for 4 to 6 hours, adding more briquets when necessary, or until the meat pulls away from the ends of the bone. Serve with your favorite barbecue sauce.

Note: You can slow smoke the rib meat scraps, along with your ribs, for use in beans and other side dishes.

SERVES 4

Sweet Stuff Glazed Baby Back Ribs

Baby backs are also called loin ribs since they are cut from the loin section of the pig. The bones are shorter than on spareribs and are slightly curved instead of straight. They tend to be meatier and more tender than spareribs. Prepackaged baby backs are already trimmed, saving you a preparation step. What's not to like? Contest barbecuers know the value of a good glaze on ribs, which involves brushing on a sweet barbecue sauce during the last 30 minutes of slow smoking. A glaze adds an attractive sheen to the ribs rather than a granular, crusty appearance. For baby backs as well as spareribs, I prefer to use fruitwood, hickory, or pecan. With the long smoking time, this is not a practical recipe for a gas grill. You can't go wrong with classic side dishes: barbecued beans, potato salad, and coleslaw.

Suggested wood:
Apple, cherry, hickory, or pecan

INGREDIENTS

2 full slabs baby back ribs

2 tablespoons freshly ground black pepper

1 teaspoon fine sea salt

¾ cup wood chips, soaked in water and drained

1 cup sweet, tomato-based barbecue sauce of your choice

METHOD

1. To skin baby back ribs, use a table knife, screwdriver, or the handle of a teaspoon to push under the membrane and lift it enough for you to get a grip on it. Pull the membrane off with needlenose pliers or a wad of paper towels and discard. Removing the membrane makes for more tender ribs and allows the smoke to penetrate the meat better. It's okay if some remains.

2. Season the ribs with the pepper and salt and place them in your rib rack, if you are using one. Set aside.

3. Fill your charcoal chimney with briquets, set the chimney on the bottom grill grate, and light, or prepare a fire in your smoker. Oil the grill grate.

4. When the coals are ready, dump them into the bottom of your grill, and spread them evenly across half. Scatter the wood chips on the hot coals. Place the ribs across from the coals on the indirect-heat side of the grill, racked or stacked if necessary. If your rib rack is too high for the lid to fit all the way down when the ribs are racked, arrange the coals on both sides of the bottom of the grill and place the rack in the middle of the grill grate. Be sure to position the rib rack so that rib meat is not directly above the hot coals. When the smoke starts to rise, close the lid. Place a candy thermometer in the lid vent.

5. Smoke the ribs at 225° to 250°F for 2 to 3 hours, or until the meat pulls away from the ends of the bone. When the ribs are done, brush both sides with the barbecue sauce and return them to the indirect-heat side of the grill, close the lid, and cook for 10 to 15 minutes more, or until the glaze has set and the ribs have a sheen. Serve with extra barbecue sauce at the table.

SERVES 4

Slow-Smoked Country-Style Ribs

Country-style ribs are thick, boneless loin strips from the blade end near the shoulder. Although sold as "ribs," they are not true ribs. They are easy to cook, though, and yield tender, flavorful, boneless meat. This recipe showcases another barbecue technique—slathering a meat and then sprinkling on a basic salt-and-pepper rub. This slather/rub combination helps make a tasty bark (also known as a crust or coating) and can also be used on brisket, pork shoulder, pork loin, or fish fillets. For the best bark, let the slather/rub stand on the food at room temperature for about 20 minutes or until it gets tacky. To stand up to the tanginess of the slather and rub, I like to use a medium-smoke wood such as hickory or pecan. The longer smoking time precludes using a gas grill for this recipe.

Suggested wood:
Hickory or pecan

INGREDIENTS

6 pounds country-style ribs

1 cup prepared yellow mustard

2 tablespoons freshly ground black pepper

1 teaspoon fine sea salt

¾ cup wood chips, soaked in water and drained

METHOD

1. Slather the meat completely with the mustard and sprinkle with the pepper and salt; set aside so that the slather becomes tacky while you build the fire.

2. Fill your charcoal chimney with briquets, set the chimney on the bottom grill grate, and light, or prepare a fire in your smoker. Oil the grill grate.

3. When the coals are ready, dump them into the bottom of your grill, and spread them evenly across half. Scatter the wood chips on the hot coals. Place the ribs on the indirect-heat side of the grill. When the smoke starts to rise, close the lid. Place a candy thermometer in the lid vent.

4. Smoke the ribs at 225° to 250°F for 3 to 4 hours, or until tender, adding more briquets when necessary. Check for tenderness by pulling a piece of meat off and tasting it.

SERVES 10

Lotsa Bark Barbecued Pork Shoulder

Formerly a Southern barbecue standard, barbecued pork shoulder/ blade roast/butt is now popular in barbecue joints across America. Since shoulders are too thick for deep smoke penetration, they carry only a hint of smoke when barbecued. A good, crusty bark—the meat's dark crust—is prized by barbecue-shoulder aficionados. Getting a good bark on your butt involves starting out with a higher temperature, then lowering the heat for slow smoking. For true Southern pork shoulder, go with hickory wood. However, I prefer a fruitwood mixed with pecan. Because pork shoulder slow smokes for at least 6 hours, this isn't one to try on the gas grill.

Suggested wood:
Hickory or a combination of apple and pecan

INGREDIENTS

3 tablespoons freshly ground black pepper

1 teaspoon fine sea salt

One 5-pound (or more) bone-in pork shoulder

2 cups wood chips, soaked in water and drained

1 cup homemade or store-bought barbecue sauce (optional)

METHOD

1. Mix the pepper and salt together and rub it on all surfaces of the pork. Set aside while you build the fire.

2. Fill your charcoal chimney with briquets, set the chimney on the bottom grill grate, and light, or prepare a fire in your smoker. Oil the grill grate.

3. When the coals are ready, dump them into the bottom of your grill, and spread them evenly across half. Scatter the wood chips on the hot coals. Place the pork on the indirect-heat side of the grill across from the coals. Increase the temperature to 350°F by opening the bottom vents on your grill. When the smoke starts to rise, close the lid. Place a candy thermometer in the lid vent. Smoke for 30 to 45 minutes to get the bark started.

4. Reduce the temperature by closing the vents until you're at 225° to 250°F. Smoke the pork for 6 to 8 hours, or until tender, adding more briquets when necessary. Check for tenderness by pulling a piece of meat off and tasting it. The mark of a shoulder done to perfection is when you can remove the blade bone by pulling it out with your hand.

5. When the pork is done, set it aside in a pan for 30 minutes, then move it to a cutting board. Serve it pulled (stringy portions torn off by hand), sliced, chopped, or as a piggie sandwich (chopped or pulled pork topped with coleslaw on a bun), with sauce on the side if desired.

SERVES 10

Butt in a Bag

This variation on the traditional method has never failed me. I learned it at the Memphis in May World Championship Barbecue event more than two decades ago from an Arkansas cook. It's simple. Place a partially smoked pork butt in a paper grocery bag and finish cooking by slow smoking it. The paper absorbs some of the grease and keeps the meat from drying out. People ask me, "Won't the bag catch on fire?" The bag will be saturated with pork fat, but a bag fire hasn't happened to me yet. For true Southern pork butt, go with hickory wood. However, I like to use fruitwood—maybe even peach or cherry—mixed with pecan. Because pork butt slow smokes for at least 6 hours, this is not a recipe to try on a gas grill.

Suggested wood:
Hickory or a combination of apple, peach, or cherry and pecan

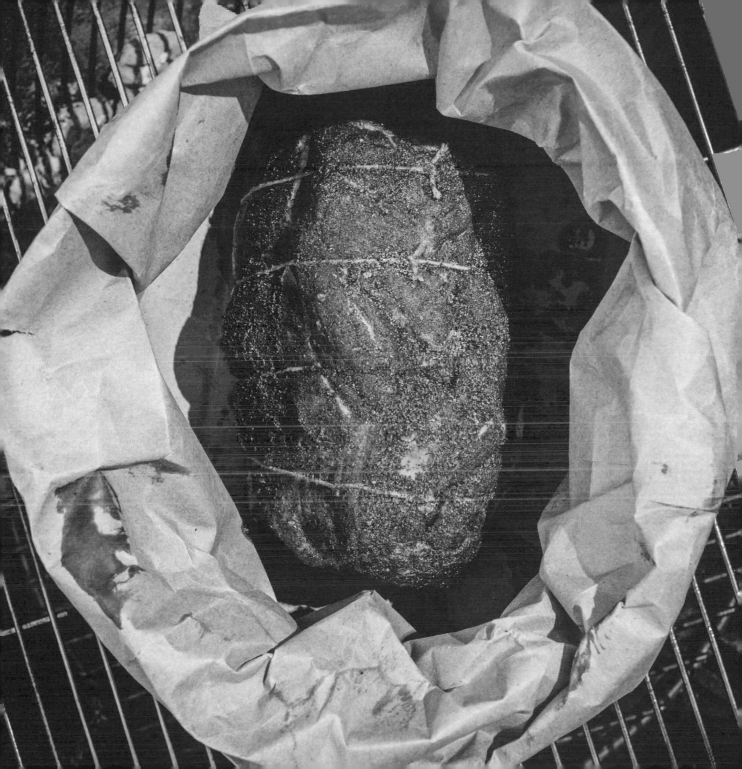

INGREDIENTS

3 tablespoons freshly ground black pepper

1 teaspoon fine sea salt

One 5-pound (or more) bone-in pork shoulder

2 cups wood chips, soaked in water and drained

Barbecue sauce of your choice (optional)

METHOD

1. Mix the pepper and salt together and rub it on all surfaces of the pork. Set aside while you build the fire.

2. Fill your charcoal chimney with briquets, set the chimney on the bottom grill grate, and light, or prepare a fire in your smoker. Oil the grill grate.

3. When the coals are ready, dump them into the bottom of your grill, and spread them evenly across half. Scatter the wood chips on the hot coals. Place the butt on the indirect-heat side of the grill across from the coals. Increase the temperature to 350°F by opening the bottom vents on your grill. When the smoke starts to rise, close the lid. Place a candy thermometer in the lid vent. Smoke for 30 to 45 minutes to get the bark started.

4. Reduce the temperature by closing the vents until you're at 225° to 250°F. Smoke the pork for 4 hours. Place the butt in a brown paper grocery bag large enough to hold it, fold the ends over to close it, and return it to the same place in the smoker, opposite the fire. Add more briquets if necessary, and close the lid. Continue smoking for 2 to 4 more hours or until tender. Check for tenderness by pulling a piece of meat off and tasting it. The mark of a shoulder done to perfection is when you can remove the blade bone by pulling it out with your hand.

5. When the shoulder is done, set it aside in a pan to rest for 30 minutes, then move it to a cutting board. Serve it Southern-style pulled (stringy portions torn off by hand), Kansas City–style thick sliced, or the-hell-with-it chopped. Some barbecuers like to mix in a little tangy barbecue sauce as they're chopping, especially if the pork is still a little fatty. Transfer to a platter and serve.

SERVES 4

Apple-Smoked Chicken Thighs

Apple smoke and apple juice spray make these chicken thighs so tasty you won't want sauce. Spraying foods with fruit juice is another trick barbecuers have in their repertoire. The sweetness in the juice counteracts the bitterness of the smoke and keeps the food moist. A fruit juice spray—usually apple or pineapple juice—is good to use on pork, chicken, or fish, of any cut or fillet, skin-on or not, bone-in or boneless. Get a plastic spray bottle from the hardware store and use it just for food purposes. Turbinado is raw sugar; if you can't find it, use light brown sugar. And here's a bonus technique—low-and-slow smoking does not make for crisp poultry skin, so right before your chicken is done, transfer it to the hot side of the grill and crisp up the skin. It's now the best of all possible worlds! Serve with potato salad and grilled or steamed fresh asparagus.

Suggested wood:
Apple

INGREDIENTS

2 cups apple juice

2 tablespoons turbinado sugar

4 large, bone-in chicken thighs, rinsed and patted dry

1 tablespoon freshly ground black pepper

1 teaspoon fine sea salt

1 cup wood chips, soaked in water and drained

METHOD

1. To make the apple juice spray, put the juice and sugar in a stainless-steel saucepan over medium heat and cook just until the sugar is dissolved. Cool to room temperature and pour into a plastic spray bottle.

2. Sprinkle the chicken thighs with the pepper and salt. Set aside while you build the fire.

3. Fill your charcoal chimney with briquets, set the chimney on the bottom grill grate, and light, or prepare a fire in your smoker. Oil the grill grate.

4. When the coals are ready, dump them into the bottom of your grill, and spread them evenly across half. Replace the grill grate. Scatter the wood chips on the hot coals. Place the chicken thighs on the indirect-heat side of the grill across from the coals and spray them with the apple juice mixture. When the smoke starts to rise, close the lid. Place a candy thermometer in the lid vent.

5. Smoke the thighs at 225° to 250°F for 1 hour, spraying the chicken every 20 minutes and re-lidding the smoker. After 1 hour, spray the chicken again, then transfer to the direct-heat side and grill over hot coals for 2 minutes, turning as necessary, or until the skin has crisped all over.

SERVES 4

This Bird's for You Beer-Can Chicken

Beer-can chicken has moved from novelty to standard fare for many backyard pitmasters. I first learned about it from the late Hank Lumpkin of Boss Hawg's BBQ in Topeka, Kansas. Hank called it "beer-butt chicken." The barbecue industry has responded with lots of beer-can chicken gadgets and holders, if you want to get fancy. You should know that once the chicken has perched on its beery throne, it never goes back to a regular roast chicken shape—the opening stays wide open. So don't plan on serving it whole on a platter; cut it into moist and delicious pieces. As the beer is mainly for the moisture and the support, don't waste a good microbrew on this recipe. I use cheap beer and get tasty results. Serve with garlic mashed potatoes garnished with chopped parsley and a medley of grilled vegetables. This is one you can do on your gas grill.

Suggested wood:
Apple, pecan, or hickory

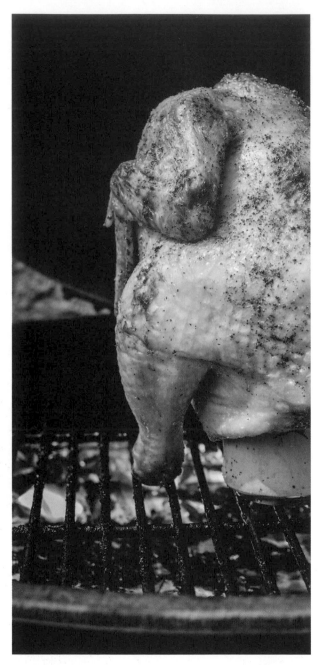

INGREDIENTS

1 cup wood chips, soaked in water and drained, or 1 cup dry chips for a gas grill

One 12-ounce can of beer

One 4-pound roasting chicken, giblets and neck removed, rinsed, and patted dry

½ cup extra-virgin olive oil

½ teaspoon fine sea salt

1 tablespoon freshly ground black pepper

Note: *The appearance of "red" meat next to the bones is a normal result of the cooking process.*

METHOD

1. Fill your charcoal chimney with briquets, set the chimney on the bottom grill grate, and light, or prepare a fire in your smoker. For a gas grill, turn the temperature to low or 250°F. Oil the grill grate.

2. When the coals are ready, dump them into the bottom of your grill, and spread them evenly across the bottom. Scatter the wood chips on the hot coals or place them in a metal container as close as possible to a burner on a gas grill.

3. Open the beer can and pour out about 1 ounce. If you're using a ceramic or stainless-steel holder with space for the beer, pour the beer into the holder. Place the chicken cavity over the beer can or holder. Place the chicken in the middle of the grill and use the chicken legs to balance it. Brush the chicken with the olive oil and sprinkle lightly with the salt and pepper. When the smoke starts to rise, close the lid. Place a candy thermometer in the lid vent of a charcoal grill or smoker.

4. Smoke at 250°F for 1½ to 2 hours, or until a meat thermometer registers 165°F when inserted into the thickest part of the thigh. Remove the chicken from the cooker and let rest, covered, for 15 minutes before carving.

SERVES 4

Wood-Smoked Rotisserie Chicken

With rotisserie cooking, the food bastes itself as it turns on the spit, for moist results. When you add a kiss of smoke, the flavor's even better. Rotisserie cooking is by nature indirect, because the spit is elevated above the heat. Although this recipe is for one chicken, many rotisserie spits have room for another chicken, so throw another one on if you're cooking for more guests or you want to have leftovers. I also like to rotisserie Cornish game hens, which take about 45 minutes. Serve with potato salad, stuffed red or orange sweet bell peppers, and buttered roasted Brussels sprouts.

Suggested wood:
Apple, pecan, or hickory

INGREDIENTS

One 4-pound roasting chicken, giblets and neck removed, rinsed, and patted dry

½ cup extra-virgin olive oil

Fine sea salt and freshly ground black pepper to taste

1 cup wood chips, soaked in water and drained, or 1 cup dry chips for a gas grill

Note: *The appearance of "red" meat next to the bones is a normal result of the cooking process.*

METHOD

1. Rub the outside and inside of the chicken with some of the olive oil. Sprinkle the chicken lightly inside and outside with salt and pepper.

2. Fill your charcoal chimney with briquets, set the chimney on the bottom grill grate, and light, or prepare a fire in your smoker. For a gas grill, turn the temperature to low or 250°F. Oil the grill grate.

3. When the coals are ready, dump them into the bottom of your grill, and spread them evenly. Scatter the wood chips on the hot coals or place them in a metal container as close as possible to a burner on a gas grill. Using long-handled tongs, grill the outside of the chicken directly over the coals, turning, until the skin is browned. Put the chicken on your rotisserie spit. Make sure it is evenly balanced on the spit.

Brush the outside of the chicken again with olive oil. When the smoke starts to rise, close the lid. Place a candy thermometer in the lid vent of a charcoal grill or smoker.

4. Smoke at 250°F for 1½ to 2 hours, or until a meat thermometer registers 165°F when inserted into the thickest part of the thigh. Remove the chicken from the cooker and let rest, covered, for 15 minutes before carving. You can also check for doneness by pulling a leg. If the leg is easy to jiggle and you don't see red blood or pink juices oozing from the chicken, the chicken is done.

SERVES 8 OR MORE

Smoked Turkey with Cranberry-Whiskey Mop

Barbecued turkey, fresh from the pit, makes a wonderful feast, and it needn't be served only once a year on a holiday. The leftovers are great in sandwiches and a variety of tasty casseroles. The secret to moist turkey is to mop it with a sweet/tart mixture like my cranberry-whiskey mop, which you apply with a cotton dish mop or grill mop or a clean cloth.

(A grill mop is a small utensil consisting of a handle and a cotton or silicone brush head used for applying basting liquids to foods while grilling. They're easy to find at your local supermarket or online.) To match the flavor, why not try wood smoke from oak barrels that have aged whiskey in them, such as Jack Daniel's whiskey-barrel wood chips? These chips are available at most big-box stores or online and only need to soak for about 15 minutes, as you don't want all that essence to leach out. If you can't find those, then apple, hickory, or pecan will still produce a fine, fine bird. Since the turkey smokes for 6 to 8 hours, this recipe is not for your gas grill. Serve with roasted sweet potatoes, fresh grilled or steamed and buttered green beans, and cornbread stuffing.

Suggested wood:
Jack Daniel's wood smoking chips or apple, hickory, or pecan

INGREDIENTS

2 cups cranberry juice

½ cup honey

⅓ cup whiskey

1 tablespoon granulated garlic

1 tablespoon freshly ground black pepper

1 teaspoon ground sage

1 teaspoon fine sea salt

One 9- to 14-pound turkey, giblets and neck removed, rinsed, and patted dry

1 cup wood chips, soaked in water and drained (if using Jack Daniel's wood chips, soak only 15 minutes)

METHOD

1. To make the mop, combine the cranberry juice, honey, whiskey, granulated garlic, pepper, sage, and salt in a medium-size bowl and whisk well.

2. Fill your charcoal chimney with briquets, set the chimney on the bottom grill grate, and light, or prepare a fire in your smoker. Oil the grill grate.

3. When the coals are ready, dump them into the bottom of your grill, and spread them evenly across half. Scatter the wood chips on the hot coals. Place the turkey, breast side up, on the indirect-heat side of the grill across from the coals. Using a cotton dish mop or grill mop, apply the cranberry-whiskey mop to the turkey. When the smoke starts to rise, close the lid. Place a candy thermometer in the lid vent of a charcoal grill or smoker.

4. Smoke at 225° to 250°F for 6 to 7 hours, adding more briquets as necessary, and mopping the bird every hour, until a meat thermometer registers 165°F when inserted into the thickest part of the thigh. Remove the turkey from the cooker and let rest, covered, for 15 minutes before carving. Turkey skin may be dark brown or black when the bird is fully cooked, but the meat inside will be moist and delicious

SERVES 4

Brown Sugar-Brined Turkey Breast

Brining is another trick that barbecuers have up their sleeves because they know that a simple mixture of salt, water, sugar, and maybe a few herbs or spices can make poultry, pork butt (the brine is injected into the thick meat), or even salmon especially juicy. I'll start you out with a simple brine that will yield succulent results—just remember to rinse the turkey breast really, really well to get rid of any extra salt after brining. Plan ahead to allow time for brining—at least 4 hours or, preferably, overnight. To brine a pork butt, strain the brine mixture, then fill a culinary injector and inject the meat all over with the brine. Gas grillers/smokers, rejoice! You can make this recipe on a gas grill. Serve with a vegetable such as corn or lima beans and a colorful salad.

Suggested wood:
Apple and pecan

INGREDIENTS

6 cups water

½ cup kosher salt

⅓ cup packed brown sugar

One 5- to 6-pound bone-in, self-basting turkey breast, rinsed and patted dry

1 cup extra-virgin olive oil

2 tablespoons honey

2 tablespoons cider vinegar

1 teaspoon freshly ground black pepper

½ teaspoon fine sea salt

1 cup wood chips, soaked in water and drained, or 1 cup dry chips for a gas grill

METHOD

1. To make the brine, combine the water, kosher salt, and brown sugar in a bowl and stir until the salt and sugar are dissolved. Place the turkey breast in a large zipper-top plastic bag or a large bowl with a cover and pour the brine over the turkey. Cover and refrigerate for 4 hours or up to overnight.

2. Fill your charcoal chimney with briquets, set the chimney on the bottom grill grate, and light, or prepare a fire in your smoker. For a gas grill, turn to low or 250°F. Oil the grill grate. Remove the turkey from the brine, discard the brine, and rinse the turkey under cold running water several times. Pat dry. In a separate bowl, mix together the olive oil, honey, vinegar, pepper, and sea salt.

3. When the coals are ready, dump them into the bottom of your grill, and spread them evenly across half. Replace the grill grate. Scatter the wood chips on the hot coals or place them in a metal container as close as possible to a burner on a gas grill. Place the turkey on the indirect-heat side of the grill across from the coals. Using a cotton dish mop or grill mop, mop the turkey with the olive oil mixture. When the smoke starts to rise, close the lid. Place a candy thermometer in the lid vent of a charcoal grill or smoker.

4. Smoke at 225° to 250°F for 4 hours, adding more briquets as necessary, and mopping the bird every hour, until a meat thermometer registers 165°F when inserted into the thickest part of the thigh. If you want the skin to be crispy, move the turkey over and grill it over hot coals or flames for 3 to 4 minutes. Remove the turkey from the cooker and let rest, covered, for 15 minutes before carving.

SERVES 4

County Fair Barbecued Turkey Legs and Thighs with Citrus Marinade

Barbecued turkey legs are a favorite at fairs, festivals, and cookouts across America because they take well to sit-down or walking-around dining. The secret to this recipe is long, slow marinating. The soy in the marinade will also darken the meat to give it a rich, mahogany finish. Use this recipe for legs, thighs, or a combo of the two. Plan ahead for at least 8 hours of marinating time. Serve with grilled corn on the cob and ice cream cones for dessert. This is another recipe you can do on a gas grill.

Suggested wood:
Apple, oak, hickory, or pecan

INGREDIENTS

½ cup extra-virgin olive oil

¼ cup soy sauce

¼ cup freshly squeezed orange juice

2 tablespoons freshly squeezed lemon juice

1 teaspoon freshly ground black pepper

1 teaspoon granulated garlic

4 turkey legs or thighs

1 cup wood chips, soaked in water and drained

Barbecue sauce of your choice for serving

METHOD

1. To make the marinade, combine the olive oil, soy sauce, orange juice, lemon juice, pepper, and granulated garlic in a bowl or a large zip per-top plastic bag and mix well. Add the turkey, cover or seal, and let marinate in the refrigerator for 8 hours or overnight.

2. Fill your charcoal chimney with briquets, set the chimney on the bottom grill grate, and light, or prepare a fire in your smoker. For a gas grill, turn to low or 250°F. Oil the grill grate. Remove the turkey from the marinade, discard the marinade, and pat dry.

3. When the coals are ready, dump them into the bottom of your grill, and spread them evenly across half. Replace the grill grate. Scatter the wood chips on the hot coals or place them in a metal container as close as possible to a burner on a gas grill. Place the turkey on the grill grate on the indirect-heat side across from the coals. When the smoke starts to rise, close the lid. Place a candy thermometer in the lid vent of a charcoal grill or smoker.

4. Smoke at 225° to 250°F for 2 hours or until a meat thermometer registers 165°F when inserted into the thickest part of the thigh. If you want the skin to be crispy, grill it over hot coals or flames for 3 to 4 minutes. Remove the turkey from the cooker and let rest, covered, for 15 minutes before carving. Slather lightly with your favorite barbecue sauce and serve.

SERVES 4

Fruitwood-Smoked Duck with Cider-Honey Mop

Thanks to Burt Culver of Culver Farms in Indiana, farm-raised domestic duck has made its way into the mainstream of barbecue entrées. Because ducks are naturally fattier than chickens and turkeys, you'll need a drip pan beneath the duck to prevent a pit fire. Fill the pan with liquid— water, vinegar, beer, or whatever you like—and place it on the bottom of your grill next to the coals. The steam from this drip pan also helps keep food moist—some barbecuers use a drip or water pan with everything they barbecue. I like to cook duck over fruitwood, as the sweet smoke matches the sweetness of the meat. Serve this with cannellini beans and chopped red bell pepper tossed together in a vinaigrette, and grilled or steamed fresh asparagus.

Suggested wood:
Apple, pecan, or cherr

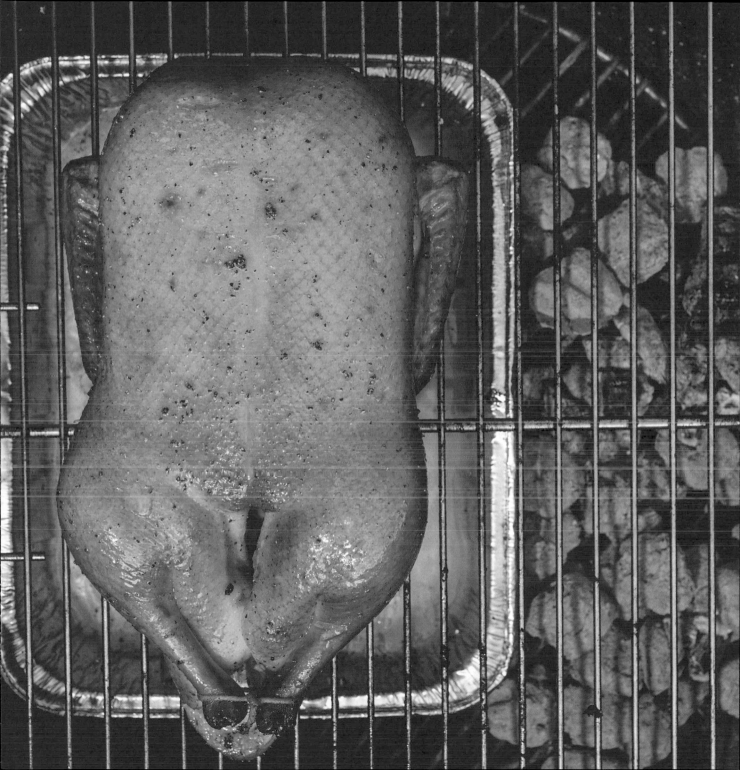

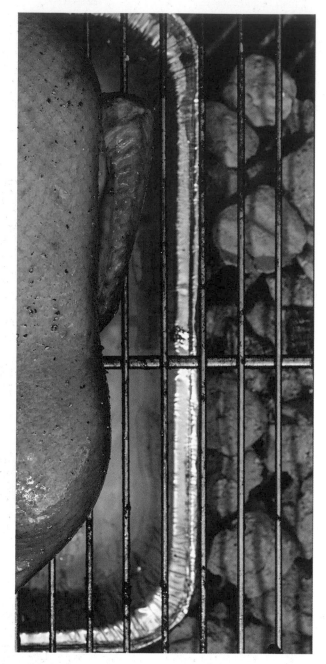

INGREDIENTS

½ cup honey

½ cup cider vinegar

2 tablespoons melted unsalted butter

2 teaspoons freshly ground black pepper

1 teaspoon fine sea salt

One 5-pound farm-raised Pekin duck (if frozen, thaw overnight in the refrigerator), giblets and neck removed, rinsed, and patted dry

1 cup wood chips, soaked in water and drained, or 1 cup dry chips for a gas grill

Orange slices for garnish

Thyme sprigs for garnish

METHOD

1. To make the mop, combine the honey, vinegar, butter, pepper, and salt in a bowl until well blended. Set aside.

2. Fill your charcoal chimney with briquets, set the chimney on the bottom grill grate, and light, or prepare a fire in your smoker. For a gas grill, turn to low or 250°F. Oil the grill grate.

3. When the coals are ready, dump them into the bottom of your grill, and spread them evenly across half. Place a disposable aluminum pan in the bottom of your grill opposite the hot coals. Fill the pan half full with water, vinegar, or beer. Replace the grill grate. Place the duck on the grill grate over the drip pan, breast side up, on the indirect-heat side. For a gas grill, place the drip pan on the grill grate on the indirect-heat side and place the duck on a roasting rack in the drip pan; partially fill the pan with liquid so that the liquid does not touch the duck. Scatter the wood chips on the hot coals or place them in a metal container as close as possible to a burner on a gas grill. Close the lid.

4. Smoke at 225° to 250°F for 2½ hours, mopping the duck with the honey-vinegar mop each half hour, adding more briquets as necessary, until a meat thermometer inserted into the thickest part of the thigh registers 180°F. When done, the leg will be loose at the joint and the skin will pull back from the tip of the leg. If you're uncertain whether the meat is done, make a small cut near the leg at the hip socket. If the meat is pink, cook the duck for another 30 minutes, or until the meat is no longer pink.

5. Remove the duck from the grill to a serving platter. Let the duck rest for 5 to 10 minutes, then carve and serve, garnished with the orange slices and thyme sprigs. Beneath the layers of skin and fat, you'll find tender, moist, delicious meat.

SERVES 6

Pitmaster's Secret Recipe Beans

Smoke a casserole? You betcha. Paul Kirk taught me a few barbecued-bean secrets years ago at a Kansas City Barbeque Society Spring Training cook-off. Over the years I have tweaked this recipe, and I encourage you to do the same. Savvy barbecuers freeze smoked meat scraps to use in dishes like this one. For casseroles such as baked beans that really only need to have their flavors blend, smoking low and slow is the way to go.

I like to smoke casseroles made from foods that are already cooked, like a baked potato casserole or a cheesy corn bake, so you're only warming them and giving them a hit of smoke in the grill. For casseroles involving foods that actually need to be cooked, like a casserole with raw potatoes, use the smoke-baking technique on page 28. You can't go wrong with KC Masterpiece Classic Blend, Bone Suckin' Original, or Rufus Teague Honey Sweet barbecue sauces in this recipe. You can smoke these beans on a gas grill, too.

Suggested wood:
Hickory

INGREDIENTS

2 tablespoons bacon grease or canola oil

1 medium-size sweet onion, chopped

2 red, orange, or green bell peppers, seeded and chopped

Five 15-ounce cans pork and beans, rinsed and drained

One 15-ounce can creamed corn

One 4-ounce can diced green chiles

2 cups chopped barbecued meat scraps (pork, beef, or a combo)

2 cups sweet, tomato-based barbecue sauce (homemade or store-bought)

Beer or cola, if necessary

METHOD

1. Add the bacon grease to a skillet and sauté the onions and peppers over medium heat until tender, about 5 minutes. Combine the beans, corn, chiles, meat, and onion-and-pepper mixture in a roasting pan. Stir in the barbecue sauce. Thin, if necessary, with beer or cola.

2. Fill your charcoal chimney with briquets, set the chimney on the bottom grill grate, and light, or prepare a fire in your smoker. For a gas grill, turn half the burners to medium.

3. When the coals are ready, dump them into the bottom of your grill, and spread them evenly across half. Scatter the wood chips on the hot coals or place them in a metal container as close as possible to a burner on a gas grill. Place the roasting pan with the beans on the indirect-heat side. Close the lid.

4. Smoke at 225° to 250°F for 2½ hours or until the casserole is bubbling and has a good, smoky aroma. You can also bake this indoors in the oven, covered, for 2 hours at 250°F.

SERVES 4

Smoke-Roasted Rustic Root Vegetables

If you can smoke bake a casserole, then you can also smoke roast. Smoke-roasted root vegetables take on smoke flavor at a higher temperature, generally around 350°F. If you like roasted vegetables in the oven, you'll love these. As an alternative method, you can also partially slow smoke vegetables, then transfer them indoors to your oven to finish roasting and crisping at a higher temperature. Substitute other root vegetables, such as parsnips, beets, turnips, and rutabagas, if you like. This recipe works well in a gas grill, too.

Suggested wood:
Cherry, oak, or pecan

INGREDIENTS

2 large carrots, cut into 2-inch chunks

2 medium-size unpeeled russet potatoes,
cut into 2-inch chunks

2 medium-size unpeeled sweet potatoes,
cut into 2-inch chunks

¼ cup extra-virgin olive oil, plus more for drizzling

Fine sea salt and freshly ground black pepper

2 tablespoons chopped fresh flat-leaf parsley,
for garnish

METHOD

1. Toss the vegetables with the olive oil and and season with salt and pepper to taste. Place the mixture on an 8 x 12-inch piece of heavy-duty aluminum foil or in a disposable aluminum pan.

2. Fill your charcoal chimney with briquets, set the chimney on the bottom grill grate, and light, or prepare a fire in your smoker. For a gas grill, turn half the burners to medium.

3. When the coals are ready, dump them into the bottom of your grill, and spread them evenly across half. Scatter the wood chips on the hot coals or place them in a metal container as close as possible to a burner on a gas grill. Place the vegetables on the indirect-heat side. Close the lid.

4. Smoke at 350°F for 45 to 60 minutes or until the potatoes are tender and the vegetables have a good, smoky aroma. Transfer the vegetables to a platter, drizzle with a little more olive oil if desired, and garnish with the chopped parsley.

Measurement Equivalents

OVEN TEMPERATURE CONVERSIONS

°F	°C	Gas Mark
250	120	½
275	140	1
300	150	2
325	165	3
350	180	4
375	190	5
400	200	6
425	220	7
450	230	8
475	240	9
500	260	10
550	290	Broil

Note: *All conversions are approximate*

WEIGHT CONVERSIONS

U.S./U.K.	Metric
½ oz	14 g
1 oz	28 g
1½ oz	43 g
2 oz	57 g
2½ oz	71 g
3 oz	85 g
3½ oz	100 g
4 oz	113 g
5 oz	142 g
6 oz	170 g
7 oz	200 g
8 oz	227 g
9 oz	255 g
10 oz	284 g
11 oz	312 g
12 oz	340 g
13 oz	368 g
14 oz	400 g
15 oz	425 g
1 lb	454 g

LIQUID CONVERSIONS

U.S.	Metric
1 tsp	5 ml
1 tbs	15 ml
2 tbs	30 ml
3 tbs	45 ml
¼ cup	60 ml
⅓ cup	75 ml
⅓ cup + 1 tbs	0 ml
⅓ cup + 2 tbs	100 ml
½ cup	20 ml
⅔ cup	50 ml
¾ cup	180 ml
¾ cup + 2 tbs	200 ml
1 cup	240 ml
1 cup + 2 tbs	275 ml
1¼ cups	300 ml
1⅓ cups	325 ml
1½ cups	350 ml
1⅔ cups	375 ml
1¾ cups	400 ml
1¾ cups + 2 tbs	450 ml
2 cups (1 pint)	475 ml
2½ cups	600 ml
3 cups	720 ml
4 cups (1 quart)	945 ml
	(1,000 ml is 1 liter)

Resources

BARBECUE AND GRILL MANUFACTURERS

Weber-Stephen Products Company
www.weber.com

Manufacturer of the icon of backyard cooking, the kettle grill, plus a variety of other smokers, grills, and accessories. Search the company's website for the grill that suits you, then buy it locally.

Primo Grills and Smokers
www.primogrill.com

This company offers top-quality oval-shaped thick ceramic grills and smokers plus accessories, all made in the U.S.A. Check out the company's products on its website, then search for a local dealer to buy.

Big Green Egg
www.biggreenegg.com

This firm sells a line of very popular egg-shaped thick ceramic grills and smokers. Find the nearest dealer via the company's website.

Viking Range Corporation
www.vikingrange.com

This maker of high-end, high-quality kitchen ranges also sells outdoor and indoor grills, smokers, and other outdoor cooking tools, all made in the U.S.A.

Horizon Smoker Company
www.horizonbbqsmokers.com

This maker of top-quality backyard, commercial, and trailer-mounted smokers has one for every occasion. Contact the company's president and owner, Roger Davidson, for information and dealer locations.

Ace of Hearts BBQ Specialties, LLC
www.thegood-one.com

Seller of The Good-One grills and smokers, introduced in 1988 in Burns, Kansas, by Ron and Larry Goodwin. See the company's website for dealer information.

Cookshack, Inc.
www.cookshack.com

Known for quality products and great customer service since the early 1960s, Cook-shack builds and sells high-quality electric/ wood smoke barbecue cookers, along with an all-wood barbecue rig and a complete line of accessories, woods, and seasonings.

BBQ Pits by Klose
www.bbqpits.com

If your dream is to own a custom-made pit built to your own specifications, David Klose is the man to contact. He's a genius at building creative, functional, top-quality, award-winning barbecue pits. David is also the man to see for standard-design grills and smokers. Check his inventory at the company's website.

Pitts and Spitts
www.pittsandspitts.com

My friend the late Jim Quessenberry cooked one of the finest hogs I've ever eaten in a Pitts and Spitts barbecue pit. In business for more than a quarter of a century, this company offers stainless-steel "restaurant grade" pits.

Char-Broil
www.charbroil.com

A leading manufacturer of quality, affordable grills, barbecue pits, and grilling accessories since 1948, Char-Broil offers its products both in local retail stores and through its website.

BARBECUE SEASONINGS

Vanns Spices Ltd.
www.vannsspices.com

Vanns offers a wide array of herbs, spices, and seasoning blends, including a line of organic spices and custom spice blends.

Zach's Spice Company
www.zachspice.com

You'll find only the freshest products at this reliable source, which specializes in spices and seasonings used in smoking, grilling, sausage making, and barbecue sauces.

WOOD PRODUCTS

Search for local sources first, including orchards that may sell or give away pruned branches from fruit, pecan, or hickory trees.

Chigger Creek Products
www.chiggercreek.com

This company sells a wide variety of woods as chips, chunks, or logs.

BBQr's Delight
www.bbqrsdelight.com

This company sells wood pellets for barbecuing.

Index

About the Author

Ardie A. Davis is an award-winning barbecue expert and the founder of Greasehouse University—the fabled institution behind the coveted degree of Ph.B., or doctor of barbecue philosophy. (The rigorous "degree program" is now overseen by the Kansas City Barbecue Society.) Sporting a bowtie and a bowler hat, Ardie judges on the barbecue circuit under the moniker Remus Powers, Ph.B. He was named a Kansas City Barbecue Legend by the *Kansas City Star* in 2003; he also writes a monthly column in the *National Barbecue News* and the *Kansas City Bullsheet*. Ardie lives with his wife, Gretchen, in the Kansas City area.

Frank Boyer